Remember

October 28, 2005

Alicia K. Lloyd

REMEMBER

Printed for distribution by Alicia K. Lloyd

and Missions in Haiti Inc.

PO Box 2996

Claremore, OK 74017

All scriptures are from the King James Version

Bible.

All definitions are from *Merriam-Webster* online

dictionary.

© 2016 Alicia K. Lloyd

All rights reserved.

ISBN: 9781530207527

Library of Congress Control Number: 2016916968

REMEMBER

Dedicated to the children:

Miriam Joanne Merenvil

Hannah Elisabeth Kay Lloyd

David Joseph Lloyd III

October 2015

REMEMBER

Contents

Author's Note

Introduction

Part I—Recall

Chapter 1

Chapter 2

Chapter 3

Chapter 4

Chapter 5

Part II—Remember

Chapter 6

Chapter 7

Chapter 8

Chapter 9

Chapter 10

Chapter 11

REMEMBER

Chapter 12

Chapter 13

Chapter 14

Chapter 15

Chapter 16

Chapter 17

Chapter 18

Part III—Reaping

Chapter 19

Chapter 20

Chapter 21

Chapter 22

Chapter 23

Chapter 24

Chapter 25

Chapter 26

Chapter 27

REMEMBER

Chapter 28

Chapter 29

Chapter 30

Appendix: Articles by the Associated Press

Author's Note

Forgetting those things which are behind, and reaching forth unto those things which are before, I press toward the mark for the prize of the high calling of God in Christ Jesus.

—Philippians 3:13b–14

It has actually been very difficult for me to write this book. Dredging up those painful memories has not been easy, but I feel that I have been able to move forward by the grace of God. As we travel to different churches, we are often asked about the kidnapping. Initially, I cringed every time someone would ask about it. The first summer we intenerated after the kidnapping, it was very hard

REMEMBER

for me to sit through service after service as my husband, David, recounted what exactly had happened. So many churches had prayed for us, and they wanted to hear the great story of God's deliverance. I can't say that I blame them.

Thankfully, after ten-plus years, I have reached the point where I can hear about it and talk about it, yet it does not bother me. But while sitting for hours at a time working on this book, sometimes a spirit of depression would settle on me.

So, it is with great relief that I have finished the recounting of that horrible October day and the dark days that followed. This book is meant to be a testimony that *nothing is impossible* for God. It is also for those Christians who struggle with feelings of despair to know that we can be overcomers through the power of God!

REMEMBER

I consider Philippians 3:13–14 to be my life verses: "Forgetting those things which are behind, and reaching forth unto those things which are before, I press toward the mark for the prize of the high calling of God in Christ Jesus."

These verses were tacked on the wall of my dorm room in college, and I decided that I would use these verses to help me to always keep my eyes on reality, which is eternal life. So, while it is good to remember what God has done, it is also good to be able to put it behind you and press forward.

REMEMBER

Introduction

And Jesus said unto him, No man, having put his hand to the plough, and looking back, is fit for the kingdom of God.

—Luke 9:62

It seems like yesterday, and it seems like forever ago, that I boarded a plane in Tulsa, Oklahoma, to come to Port-au-Prince, Haiti, for my first term. At that time, you could still wait at the gate to see people off. Many friends from church and family came to help us on our way.

Tears were streaming down my face, and I was afraid of what lie ahead. As we started down

REMEMBER

the hall toward the plane, I felt like my breathing was getting faster, and I turned to David and told him I could not go; I could not do it. He told me it was too late; I had already made a commitment.

I have always wanted to give God my best effort, though at times I know I fall miserably short. But sometimes when the going gets rough—and I look back at what and who I have left behind—I remember what Jesus said in Luke 9:62: "And Jesus said unto him, No man, having put his hand to the plough, and looking back, is fit for the kingdom of God."

People often ask David and me if we would have gone to Haiti if we had known all that would happen while we were there. Our response is that we probably could not have handled it if we had known all that lay ahead. That is why God gives

REMEMBER

grace for every situation and helps us to face one day at a time. It is also why you must be assured of your calling and be committed to it so that no matter what happens you will see it through.

REMEMBER

PART I—RECALL

First Prayer Card, 1998

> REMEMBER

Chapter 1

Recall

(to remember something from the past)

This I recall to my mind, therefore have I hope.

—*Lamentations 3:21*

You might wonder how we ended up in Haiti. Well, let me tell you.

What I have seen throughout my life is that God speaks through circumstances that come our way. Of course, we need to seek God in prayer and ask him to help us to discern his plan and calling for our lives. But we must realize he also uses the circumstances of our lives to help us to become the people who he can use to do his will.

REMEMBER

It's really kind of strange: Christians may be shocked by the audacity of atheists and atheism, but we ourselves often act as if there is no God. We may complain and get upset over the uncontrollable events in our lives. We often act as if we're just here by chance, left to sort life out on our own with no guidance or direction.

In fact, what happens to you that is out of your control is God's will for your life. God is in charge of everything! God is in charge of our lives. And the events that he allows, such as getting the families we were born into, settling in the towns in which we live, and possessing our skill sets, talents, and gifts are all part of God's divine blueprint for our success.

God works through open doors and opportunities. Many see the will of God for their

REMEMBER

lives as something mysterious and deep. But really, it is simple. If it is your heart's desire to do God's will—go out, start doing something for God or preparing to do something, and God will direct you. He will begin to open doors that will show you what all he has for you.

I was born on a snowy spring day, March 21, 1974, in the small college town of Alva, Oklahoma. I was the first child of Mike and Wanda McCrate. By the time I was six months old, we had moved to Perryton, Texas, where my dad began his career in the farm equipment business. In 1979, my dad was transferred to Guymon, Oklahoma, where I started kindergarten and nearly finished first grade before my dad was once again transferred, this time to Dodge City, Kansas.

REMEMBER

My mom always took us to church. In the summer of 1983 at vacation Bible school, I gave my heart to God. I was so excited! My mom had come to pick me up, and I ran out and told her I had given my heart to God.

The churches I attended in Kansas, and later in Oklahoma, had a big influence on my desire to work for God. They encouraged people to read missionaries' biographies and autobiographies from the mission books you could borrow that were always on a table in the foyer. When you were finished, you signed your name on the front inside cover; there was a competition to see how many you could read and how many times a book had been signed.

REMEMBER

I was enthralled by these stories, and I wanted to be like the missionaries I was reading about. I believed my life could make a difference in the lives of others.

After graduating from Claremore High School in 1992, I didn't have a specific plan or direction for my life. I knew that I wanted to do something to help lead the lost to a relationship with God. I decided I would become a nurse; I figured that would be a good career, as well as a way I could do what I felt I should be doing. I enrolled in Rogers State College in Claremore, Oklahoma.

As my first year of college progressed, I was discontented and felt a yearning in my heart. The truth is I was allowing the enemy to confuse me, and that left me without direction. But God had a

REMEMBER

plan for my life, and it was time for me to start taking specific steps toward that plan.

As the school year was coming to a close, I went with a friend to a mission conference in Sand Springs, Oklahoma, at Vernon Jarvis's church. Robert Holmes, the speaker that night, was on furlough from Africa. He talked about being a teacher at Ozark Bible Institute, and I found his stories very compelling. I went to the altar and prayed. I felt God direct me to enroll in Bible school in Neosho, Missouri, where I believed he would direct my future path. I felt clarity and excitement for the first time in a long time!

> REMEMBER

Chapter 2

Ridicule

(harsh comments made by people who are laughing at someone or something)

But God hath chosen the foolish things of the world to confound the wise; and God hath chosen the weak things of the world to confound the things which are mighty.
—*1 Corinthians 1:27*

The book of Nehemiah is one of the Old Testament books that shows the need for great faith and courage and gives lessons on prayer and confidence in the middle of trials. It is a great book of revival about working for God with some tremendous character-building truths, and it gives

REMEMBER

many examples of victory. This book shows us that Nehemiah had a great vision to work for God; he had a vision of the need, of what God could do, and of his own place in God's work. Nehemiah's burden grew as he prayed and fasted while God prepared Nehemiah's heart to be willing to do what needed to be done in the future.

Unfortunately, in chapter 4, verses 1–2, Sanballat heard that the Jews were going to rebuild the wall. This made him angry, and he began to ridicule them. "When Sanballat heard that we builded the wall, he was wroth, and took great indignation, and mocked the Jews. And he spake before his brethren and the army of Samaria, and said, what do these feeble Jews? Will they fortify themselves? Will they sacrifice? Will they make an

REMEMBER

end in a day? Will they revive the stones out of the heaps of the rubbish which are burned?"

Just as Nehemiah faced ridicule when it became known that he was going to rebuild the wall, so I faced ridicule when I shared that I would be leaving my nursing studies and going to Bible college. My decision to leave behind a scholarship and a career path that would give me a good future—trading all that for a Bible college education with no certainty about what I would do with the future—was indeed seen by many friends and family as ludicrous.

I worked at Home Medical Services after college each day during the spring semester and full time during the summer. As I had worked there for over a year, I knew I needed to share my plans so the company could start recruiting my replacement.

REMEMBER

The boss was very angry and told me what a foolish decision I was making and that I would regret it. He wanted to know what I was thinking. He went through the process of telling me about the job security I would have as a nurse, and that I would have no job security by choosing ministry as a profession. It was all I could do to listen; I knew I had to do what God had lain on my heart.

In retrospect, I am glad that God gave me the faith and courage to follow where he was leading me. You will be happiest and full of joy when you are in the middle of God's will and plan!

REMEMBER

Chapter 3

Reassure

(to make someone feel less afraid, upset, or doubtful)

And hereby we know that we are of the truth, and shall assure our hearts before him.

—1 John 3:19

If I didn't believe that God had specifically called me to be a missionary, it would be difficult, if not impossible, to survive the stress of being in the ministry. Often I feel tempted to leave Haiti, and it is only the reassurance that I have a call from

REMEMBER

God—and my commitment to that call—that keeps me here.

I felt God touch my heart to be a missionary on February 15, 1994, in dorm devotions. Linda Holmes, a missionary to Africa, came and spoke to us. During prayer time, I can say that God spoke to my heart—specifically telling me it was his will that I become a missionary.

A month later on March 16, God reconfirmed this call to me during a chapel service. He spoke to me that it was he who had chosen me. What I felt was not of man or myself, but from God, the Creator. I was not to think someone else would go; in other words, I was not to shrug this off and feel that, if I didn't do it, someone else would.

> REMEMBER

Chapter 4

Romance

(an emotional attraction)

Two are better than one; because they have a good reward for their labour. For if they fall, the one will lift up his fellow: but woe to him that is alone when he falleth; for he hath not another to help him up.

—Ecclesiastes 4:9–10

REMEMBER

David Lloyd arrived at Ozark Bible Institute in the fall of 1994. We had some classes together and were in Latin America prayer bands. I never really thought too much about him until one day when he got up to give a country report in prayer bands. Each week, a student would present such a report to help us better pray for specific countries in the Latin America region. As David began to speak, his voice went up several octaves as he nervously began—I felt really sorry for him. I was surprised to hear him say he was going to be a missionary to Haiti.

After that we talked more often, and we ended up going to the spring banquet together. I did understand that pursuing this relationship meant

REMEMBER

that, when we married, we would go to Haiti. And, as they say, the rest is history!

After I graduated in April of 1997, we married on May 30. Our first trip to Haiti was in April of 1998. David received his diploma in 1998 after completing his courses via correspondence. We began intenerating on the weekends to go full time in September of 1998.

Chapter 5

Rejoice

(an instance, occasion, or expression of joy)

Lo, children are an heritage of the Lord: and the fruit of

the womb is his reward.

—Psalm 127:3

When I first came to Haiti, I was incredibly lonely. At the time, e-mail was becoming popular

REMEMBER

for which I will forever be grateful because phone calls were still very costly. In fact, to call my mom, after an international connection fee, it cost about eighty-five cents a minute.

I used to stare at an airplane overhead, and my heart would squeeze in my chest with the pain of homesickness. I would count the days until I could go see my mom and dad and family. I wanted to do what God had asked me, but it was sure lonely.

When God blessed me with children, most of the homesickness left. I then had someone who needed my attention, and I knew it was my responsibility to build a life for them. It was literally one of the best things that ever happened to me!

I am blessed to have three beautiful, healthy biological children. I am also blessed with the

REMEMBER

privilege of raising many Haitian children as my own.

July 3, 2000, and April 2, 2002, were very blessed indeed; these were the days that Davy and Hannah were born. They are specified here as this story I am telling is theirs as well.

I had wanted to be a mother my whole life—ask my brother and sister, Tim McCrate and Amy Barr. I always thought I was their mother whenever my mom was not around. I felt responsible to look after them and be sure they were doing what they were supposed to do, and maybe sometimes even what I wanted them to do. My youngest brother, Travis McCrate, was an exception; he didn't listen and obey me as the other two had.

The day Davy was born, I could not believe how blessed I was with this perfect little baby; he

REMEMBER

was all mine and David's. I remember lifting him up, looking at him, and thinking that he was so exceptional that he would never need to be disciplined. (I was incorrect; he isn't perfect, but he is a great kid!)

Hannah was my dream come true. She was born with a head full of thick black hair. I was so proud to have a daughter who I could dress up like a little doll, and I knew she would be my best friend forever. I was so happy! Things don't always turn out how we wish: Hannah ended up hating lace and pouffed netting; it made her itchy, and her dad would make me change her.

I also remember when each of my Haitian children came. I felt joy in my heart at the chance to change someone's life through the grace of God and help him or her realize a better future. Of course, as

REMEMBER

the children grew, I came to see how idealistic I had been. I saw that things didn't always turn out as I had imagined.

I remember the day Miriam's brother brought her to my house. He came with another lady whom I was taking to meet with an organization that took in children who were, in turn, placed for adoption. He said he didn't care what happened to her, just that he could no longer take care of her. We all went to the organization and talked to the director, who informed me that Miriam was too old to be adopted, and she could not help.

Miriam was ten years old, but she was very tiny for her age. My heart hurt for her because her brother had said he didn't care what happened to her. She was an orphan; both parents had passed away, leaving her with no one who really cared as

REMEMBER

she was the only child from her mother and father's union. All the other siblings were half brothers. I agreed to take her in.

REMEMBER

Part II—Remember

House of Compassion, November 2005

> REMEMBER

Chapter 6

Reason

(a statement or fact that explains why something is the way it is; why someone does, thinks, or says something; or why someone behaves a certain way)

Men do not despise a thief, if he steal to satisfy his soul when he is hungry.
—Proverbs 6:30

What is the reason that kidnapping is so bad in Haiti? In the past, Haiti was known to have kidnapping rings that took political, social, and even business rivals. If they could not get to the actual rival, they would then take members of the family

REMEMBER

to get their message across. However, in the year 2004, kidnapping became big business. It was not as organized as it had been in the past. Haiti's depressed economy turned many petty street criminals into kidnappers; the ransom money became a source of income used for survival. Kidnappers didn't make any distinction as far as nationality, race, gender, or age. Anyone perceived as having any kind of wealth or family abroad were considered targets.

In spite of the negative light cast on Haiti, most people in Haiti are friendly and peaceful. I think the thing that is most alarming to visitors is that Haitians tend to be loud while talking. If you do not understand the language, their conversation can be misconstrued as an argument.

REMEMBER

As I write this, travelers to Haiti are reminded of the potential for spontaneous protests and public demonstrations, especially in the Port-au-Prince area. These uprisings can result in violence. Visitors are advised to take common sense precautions; they are warned to avoid any event where crowds may congregate.

Visitors and residents must remain on alert due to the absence of an effective police force in Haiti. There is always the potential for looting, the presence of random roadblocks set by armed gangs or by the police, and the possibility of random violent crime. Kidnapping for ransom remains a serious threat as well.

Chapter 7

Remember

(to have or keep an image or idea in your mind of something or someone from the past, to think of something or someone from the past again)

And thou shalt remember all the way which the Lord thy God led thee these forty years in the wilderness, to humble thee, and to prove thee, to know what was in thine heart, whether thou wouldest keep his commandments, or no.
—*Deuteronomy 8:2*

As the ten-year anniversary of the children's kidnapping approached, I wanted to take time to

REMEMBER

remember and share some of what God has done for us over the years while we have been here in Haiti.

Haitians hate to be, as they say, "reproached." If I am reproached, I know that it is something I brought on myself and that I deserve it. Some people in Haiti see it this way, but most do not. The first time I was told, "Don't reproach me," I had to ask what it meant. Many Haitians have an inferiority complex due to poverty that they face on a daily basis. When you remind them that they are acting rudely toward you, and you do not feel it is justified because you have tried to help them, they usually reply, "Don't reproach me."

They take the verse in Mathew 6:3, "But when thou doest alms, let not thy left hand know what thy right hand doeth," to mean that you are

REMEMBER

never to remind someone of the good you have done for him or her.

Here is an example: teachers are allowed to put their children in school for free. They are also given a free uniform, and books are provided. I had one teacher who, after receiving this for three of his children, came back and asked for money to buy shoes, socks, ribbons, and barrettes for his girls. I felt awkward that he would continue to ask after all I had already been able to provide. So I simply said, "I guess you forgot that I have given them a scholarship to attend school for the year, which includes monthly tuition, books, materials, and a uniform." I figured if he remembered this he would feel ashamed to continue asking. That was not the case. He told me he didn't like it when I reproached him.

REMEMBER

As a child, I was reproached often. I now see that it was a way to suppress a spirit of ungratefulness that could build in my life. For example, when I was young, my mother took us on a back-to-school fun day. We would buy things we needed for the school year. We also got to eat lunch out, which was a big treat for us. Soon after arriving home, I started in with my typical teenager ways of complaining that I didn't have exactly what I wanted, and then when asked to help with a household chore, I would begin complaining that I was being treated unjustly and had to do *everything*.

At this point, my mother asked me how I could be so unappreciative after the great day we had spent buying things and enjoying special treats. Had I already forgotten? After all, she had put her schedule and things she needed to do on hold to

REMEMBER

make time to take me to get what I needed for school and make a special memory for me.

Of course, my mom always reminded me on such days that *you reap what you sow*. One day I had taken Mania, a young lady we were raising in our home in Haiti, out to do some shopping and have lunch with me. It was a special occasion for her. After returning home, she snarled at me when she was asked to help. I asked if what I had done for her was in vain, in that I could not ask for a little help in return for the kindness I had shown. She told me that she didn't like to be reproached.

Another time I took Nancy for a day out. Later in the day, she developed an attitude with me. I asked why she would treat me like that after all the fun we had that day. Mania asked Nancy why she would let me reproach her like that.

REMEMBER

As I remember things that have happened over the years, I have a decision to make. I can choose to have things I remember continue to hurt me, or I can take a lesson. I have seen that many people allow bad things that have happened over the years make them bitter. While this is difficult when you have been hurt deeply, I want to keep my relationship with God up to date so that he can help me turn my sorrow into happiness.

The lesson I have learned in all this is that I need to ask God to give me a spirit of humility in my life. If I am acting in such a way that someone feels obligated to reproach me, I need to listen to what he or she has to say and ask God to show me if it is true. If it is, I need to correct the wrong I have done. I have also been reminded that I do not want to have a sense of ungratefulness that often comes

REMEMBER

when we fail to remember what someone has done for us. Most importantly, I have learned to ask God to reproach me. By that, I mean I want him to remind me what he has done for me and help me to be grateful.

> REMEMBER

Chapter 8

Recount

(to relate in detail, narrate)

That I may publish with the voice of thanksgiving, and tell of all thy wondrous works.

—*Psalm 26:7*

October 28, 2005

I was sitting on the bed. Hannah squatted in front of me while I fixed her hair. She was too little to be going to school, but we let her go anyway—she wanted to be like Davy. She was fussing that her hair was fine, and I was telling her it wasn't good yet. After several attempts, I clipped on a red

REMEMBER

bow with Dalmatians on it. I could tell she was tired as it had been a long week. It was a good thing it was Friday, so she could rest that weekend.

Davy and Hannah left for school with David, and I went about my usual business, never thinking this day would be any different than yesterday. As we had just opened our second Haitian school in a small house down the road, I went down to make sure everything was running smoothly and then headed back to the house.

The day passed as usual. At two o'clock, I started getting ready to go pick up the children from school, and Miriam decided to go with me. We headed out about two fifteen. There was a lady who was walking and selling stuff as I pulled out of the gate. I asked her what she was selling, and she explained it was chocolate to make hot cocoa. I

REMEMBER

knew I would probably not use it, but I felt sorry for her, so I bought it to help her out.

On the way, David called to tell me that I did not need to come pick up the children; he would just bring them with him. I told him I was already on the way. As I arrived at the school, I saw David waiting with the children in front. I pulled up; he helped them in the car and then told us he would see us soon. He shut the door and went back in the school for his meeting. I told Davy and Hannah we had gotten a goat that day. I knew they would be excited.

As we pulled out of the exit gate, there was a white truck there waiting about halfway down the short road that would put me out onto the main road. As I neared the truck, it suddenly pulled into the middle of the road and blocked me in. I tried to

REMEMBER

swerve around the truck, but the road was too crowded, and I was stuck. The windows were tinted, so I couldn't see what was going on. A man stepped out in a police uniform with a pistol in his hand. I figured I was going to get in trouble for trying to go around him as he initially started blocking the road. I realized, immediately, that this was serious! Something was wrong because he still had his gun in his hand. I rolled down the window, and he told me to move over.

I told him if he wanted money, we would give him money! I told him if he wanted the car to let us out, and we would give him the car! I kept thinking, "If I am able to stall long enough, someone will come and help us." I saw the vehicle that had been pulling out of the gate behind me start to back in, and I realized I was on my own.

REMEMBER

I initially did not even think about this actually being a kidnapping; we had yet to hear of kidnappers going after missionaries. He insisted that I move over as he held the gun toward my head. I told him I would not move over. I assume he reached in through the window, unlocked the door, and opened it because the next thing I remember, I was on the ground. Hannah's screaming pierced my heart as they drove away with the children in my car!

At this point, the security guard at the gate fired his shotgun. Seconds later, news reached David inside the school, and he hopped in his truck. As he passed me on the road, he asked which way they had gone, but I admitted I had no idea. He drove off thinking he could catch them—I felt hopeless.

REMEMBER

I was so scared that I lost control of my bladder. I just could not think, and I kept screaming. I was later told that the screaming had lasted for at least an hour. I begged those around me not to tell my mom and dad because I knew it would break their hearts.

I was so angry! I didn't understand how this could have happened to me when I was helping to take care of so many children who were not my own, and now my own children had been taken from me.

During this time, someone had the presence of mind to realize what needed to be done and contacted the US Embassy for us. Workers at the embassy, in turn, contacted the Haitian government in order to receive permission to assist in the search

REMEMBER

and rescue of the children since two of them were US citizens.

With the permission of the host government and in conjunction with the State Department, the Federal Bureau of Investigation (FBI) deployed its resources, supporting the investigative efforts of the foreign government. The size of our overseas deployment depended on the scope of the incident and what the host government requested.

At one point, David's dad called asking for Davy. My initial reaction was that someone was trying to play a sick joke since Davy had been taken. As my head cleared, I realized it was my father-in-law asking for his son (David's nickname was Davy). I asked him if he was coming, and he told me he would.

REMEMBER

The school director, Linda Threadgill, called some friends to come get me. Tom and Bev Brumbly, along with Carole Comeau, came and got me at the school. I went with them to their house on Delmas. As I didn't want to be with anyone, I asked if I could be left alone to pray; they gave me a room.

David went around to different radio stations asking that they announce that two American children and one Haitian child had been lost, and he gave the phone number where we could be reached with information concerning them. When he felt he could do no more, he came by, got me, and we headed home.

And so started the longest night of my life. Hannah had always slept with a little cloth doll she called "Baby." Davy had slept with a blanket he

REMEMBER

called "Night Night." I remembered pinning the blanket to the doll and crying as I held on to what was dear to my children.

I was angry at God. I didn't understand how he could have allowed this to happen to me. Worst-case scenarios swirled through my head: they were dead—their tiny bodies left to rot with no final resting place and no kind words spoken over them; they were sold into a life of slavery. In any case, I would be tormented the rest of my life never knowing for sure what had happened to them or where they were.

I sat recounting all the things I had read over the years; I have always loved to read missionary biographies and autobiographies. In fact, I had just read *In the Presence of My Enemies*, by Gracia Burnham, the book about the couple from Kansas

REMEMBER

who were kidnapped in the Philippines. In this book, Burnham recounts the story of her captivity at the hands of a Muslim extremist group in the Philippines. For a little over a year, she and her husband, Martin, a missionary pilot, lived with their captors and several other hostages in the Philippine jungle. In a rescue attempt gone wrong, the Philippine Army shot and killed Martin Burnham and a nurse who was the other remaining hostage. Gracia Burnham was also shot but rescued and treated for a leg wound.

I had read about all the sacrifices that had been made for the word of God to go forward on the foreign field. I thought, "Oh no, now it is my turn, and I do not know if I can handle it."

Many missionaries have suffered the loss of children while serving God in a foreign land. The

REMEMBER

Brumblys, who had picked me up earlier, had lost an infant in a plane accident on their way back to Haiti. I know several others that have faced this too.

David and I had different ways of dealing with this situation, which led to a little more stress on my part. Immediately after receiving the news the children had been taken, David peeled out of the school drive and headed out to try to find the kids. He even ventured into the dangerous slum of Bel Air and was warned to get out before he himself was kidnapped.

Of course, David's family and my family deal with grief in completely different ways. We are very emotional and expressive, while his family tends to be reserved. Therefore, we were having some problems dealing with this situation. It became an added challenge as I realized David

REMEMBER

needed to be left alone to process as well as to remain active to feel like he was doing something to help the situation. I, on the other hand, needed someone to hold me and let me talk and cry.

> REMEMBER

Chapter 9

Resolution

(the act of determining)

But as for me and my house, we will serve the Lord.

—Joshua 24:15

After pleading with God for the return of my children—and telling him how unfair it was that *my* children had been taken—the Lord began to speak to my heart. I had made a promise that I would be a good soldier of the cross for Christ despite what came my way. I had promised that I would serve him in Haiti so that others would learn of him.

REMEMBER

I remembered Grandma and Grandpa McCrate standing at the side of the casket of their only daughter. At first, I heard Grandma say, "What a waste." Then, as if she remembered her place before God, she lifted her hand and praised God for Aunt Susie's life. This godly example struck my heart during that dark night. Everything isn't all about me, but it is about him and what can bring glory to his name.

I immediately repented of my haughty attitude and told God I was sorry for being prideful by recounting what I had done for him and Haiti. I made a resolution, and I told God that I would stay in Haiti and do what he had asked me to do no matter what the outcome. Even if I never knew what happened to my children, I would serve him in

REMEMBER

Haiti. I felt a peace sweep over my soul that everything would be fine.

I can't say that peace stayed with me; doubt would lift its ugly head from time to time reminding me of the horrors of what was taking place. I felt as if I would be overtaken in grief and fear.

David assured me we would soon hear from the kids. As I watched the sun start to rise, I became more upset as I realized the night had passed, and we still had no word from, or of, the children.

Chapter 10

Rally

(a public meeting to support or oppose someone or something)

Have pity upon me, have pity upon me, O ye my friends;

for the hand of God hath touched me.

—Job 19:21

The morning after the kidnapping, many Haitians rallied around us. I was touched by their concern and care; many had been praying and had their churches praying for the safe return of the children. I had to admit, I was a little surprised. Sometimes I felt that people in Haiti were around to

REMEMBER

see what I could give them, but this day there was nothing I could do for them. I saw that their care was genuine.

Judes Montis, who is now the national director for Missions in Haiti, had been there waiting with the Haitian children when we arrived home late the night before. He was back by six the next morning to see what he could do to help.

I had no real idea just how many people had been praying for us until this ordeal was over. We received many phone calls from family and friends in the United States letting us know they were glad to hear the children had been returned to us and that they had been praying.

REMEMBER

Chapter 11

Ring

(to sound resonantly or sonorously)

And the noise was heard afar off.

—*Ezra 3:13b*

We had been in contact with the FBI, and they had given us advice on how to negotiate as they were not available to come to Haiti until Monday. We were told that we needed to ask to talk to the children.

Around nine in the morning, we received the first ransom call, which was brief after we had established that the caller did, in fact, have the

REMEMBER

children. We were extremely relieved to have established a connection with the ones who had our children, but we told them that we had to talk to each of the three children before we would consider negotiations. David talked to the children on the phone, and they told us they were okay, but Hannah started crying. David told the kidnappers Hannah needed to come home to her momma because she was just a baby. David explained that we were here to help people and that we didn't have a lot of money. They informed David that they were aware of what we were doing here.

| REMEMBER |

Chapter 12

Rescue

(to free from confinement, danger, or evil)

O Lord, thou hast brought up my soul from the grave:

thou hast kept me alive, that I should not go down to the

pit.

—Psalm 30:3

REMEMBER

Davy, Miriam, and Hannah celebrate their safe return with a cake and gifts from Agape Flights.

I find it ironic that the pastor of our church here in La Plaine actually witnessed the rescue of our children. He was in the area, heard all the commotion, and went to see what was going on. He told us that the police had badly beaten the men who were holding our children.

REMEMBER

These men were then put in prison. Haitian police are known to mistreat suspects at the time of arrest as well as while they are being held. Most of the time they are beaten with fists, sticks, and belts. Various international organizations have documented allegations that prisoners are choked, burned with cigarettes, and hooded and hit in the ear with such intense force that it causes permanent damage. The pastor who saw our children rescued said the kidnappers received a severe beating.

> REMEMBER

Chapter 13

Reunion

(a reuniting of persons after separation)

Oh that the salvation of Israel were come out of Zion!

when the Lord bringeth back the captivity of his people,

Jacob shall rejoice, and Israel shall be glad.

—Psalm 14:7

We were led into the police station and seated. There we waited as they brought our children to us. Davy's and Hannah's cheeks were flushed, and they had mosquito bites covering them. They were a bit dehydrated, but overall, they looked okay.

| REMEMBER |

Later, they recounted how the kidnappers had been nice to them—they had even let them eat cheese puffs and drink Coca-Cola—a treat to them! Davy had some leftover lunch in his lunch box, so they were able to eat that also. They were excited about their new adventure of getting to use a bucket as a toilet.

Dave's dad had flown in, but upon finding that the situation had been resolved, he decided to head out again the next morning.

> REMEMBER

Chapter 14

Ransom

(money that has been paid in order to free someone who has been captured or kidnapped)

Even as the Son of man came not to be ministered unto,

but to minister,

and to give his life a ransom for many.

—*Matthew 20:28*

After the children were returned, the question many asked was, "How much did you have to give the kidnappers for ransom?" We were more than glad to tell that Jesus once again had paid the ransom for us by delivering our children from the hands of the kidnappers with the help of the Haitian

REMEMBER

police. Therefore, no money was exchanged with them for the return of our children.

Of course, in Haiti, as in many other places in the world, it isn't *what* you know but *who* you know. We knew a man at the time who had previously worked with some of the gangs in Haiti. He had a relationship with many of the leaders; he went to them and asked if they had the children or could help us locate them.

They did help to locate the children and then were able to give that information to the police. In return for their help, we were asked to pay a $1,000 finder's fee.

REMEMBER

Chapter 15

Realization

(the act of achieving something that was planned or hoped for)

For I know the thoughts that I think toward you, saith the Lord, thoughts of peace, and not of evil, to give you an expected end.

—*Jeremiah 29:11*

At the time of the kidnapping, we were just beginning to realize our vision for Missions in Haiti. Through the generosity of donors, we were able to purchase a piece of property in La Plaine near the Bon Repos area and had plans to begin construction. We were so excited! Until this point,

REMEMBER

we had been renting houses that were less than ideal for our children's home and for raising Haitian children.

After the kidnapping, we realized that it had been a direct attack of the enemy because we were pushing to move forward for God. Every advance that is made for the kingdom of God will be met with a setback from the enemy. The area we were moving to was surrounded by lots of voodoo. Satan does not like it when we move in on his territory.

In Ephesians, chapter 6, verse 12, we see that we are not fighting against man but rather our adversary, the devil: "For we wrestle not against flesh and blood, but against principalities, against powers, against the rulers of the darkness of this world, against spiritual wickedness in high places."

REMEMBER

An example of the blatant voodoo in our area is right down the road. There is a large tree near a creek, known as a Mapou, which is considered to be a sacred tree here in Haiti to those who practice voodoo. Ceremonies are often performed around the tree, and you can always find melted candle wax and other items left in the crevices and on the branches of the tree that have served as altars to the spirits.

Although I do not know of any voodoo priests in the area, there is a mambo, the female version of the voodoo priest. As a mambo, it is her responsibility to conduct rituals and also to maintain the relationship of the community with the spirit world. She is also in the business of recruiting others to become apprentices who can later become mambos themselves.

REMEMBER

While you may be imagining someone who is the epitome of evil, she is, in fact, polite and keeps herself well groomed. I have been in the same room with her on various occasions. When a friend of mine called me to take her to the hospital to have her baby, I knew we couldn't make it in time; they called the mambo to deliver the child.

REMEMBER

Chapter 16

Response

(something that is done as a reaction to something else)

Hear me speedily, O Lord: my spirit faileth: hide not thy face from me, lest I be like unto them that go down into the pit. Cause me to hear thy lovingkindness in the morning; for in thee do I trust: cause me to know the way wherein I should walk; for I lift up my soul unto thee.

—Psalm 143:7–8

Initially, I was so happy at the outcome of this horrible situation, and I wanted to keep a good attitude for the children. I was literally going on adrenaline. I wanted everything to appear and feel normal for the children since they didn't seem upset by what had happened.

The day after the children were rescued we went to church. I remember people greeting me at the door, asking me what I was doing there. They said I needed a break, but I told them I had to keep everything going so the children would feel a sense of normalcy.

That year, we decided to go home early for the holidays. We left in November so that we could spend Thanksgiving with our families; we planned to be there through January at which time David would need to be back for the second semester of school.

We were in the Saint Louis area visiting David's family when we got a call from the FBI;

REMEMBER

they wanted to investigate our situation. We were somewhat taken aback, as a month had already passed, and we were trying to move on. They were actually in Haiti, and they wanted to meet with us.

We explained that we were in the States. They had Judes take Miriam to the Hotel Montana, where they could interview her, and then told us to be in Washington, DC, on Monday morning so they could speak with us. This somewhat messed up our plans, but we agreed to go.

During this week, we rehashed what had taken place. I was even asked to identify the kidnapper. I told them there was no way that I could; if I had been asked right after it happened maybe I could have, but, at this point, it was impossible. I looked through their books with mug shots. I also explained that the man who held the

REMEMBER

gun to me was not caught with the children; he had passed them off before they had been rescued.

I was told that if the kidnappers were identified and arrested, they could be brought to the United States to stand trial, and if they were found guilty, they would serve thirty years for each American child they had kidnapped. I had heard about the conditions of the Haitian jail and knew that if they came to the States, it would be a luxury.

In Haiti, conditions in the jails are appalling; some have compared the jails to a slave ship. In one twelve-by-fifteen-foot cement cell, there has been known to be up to forty men. They are forced to sit one behind the other in tight rows, knees to chins. There is no room to lie down.

There is no toilet or sink. In order to use a toilet, the prisoner must use a bag to defecate in; the

REMEMBER

bag will then be tied and thrown out a window. If they need to urinate, there is a community bucket that stays inside the cell and, more often than not, is overflowing.

I have been told that the cells are sometimes pitch black due to the lack of electricity, and the air is thick with the scent of human sweat and waste. The heat is stifling for the prisoners who are packed in like this with no fan or air conditioner. There are no chairs, beds, or mats to sleep on or sit on. No food is provided to the prisoners; they must depend on a family member to bring them food.

Tap water is supposed to be accessible, but such water has not been purified and is another factor that puts everyone at high risk. Tap water can typically transmit typhoid fever, hepatitis, parasites, and amoebas. Improperly washing and drying

REMEMBER

clothes can lead to fungal infections or parasitic infestations that quickly become open and infected sores. There is no medical care provided.

To me, this was a description of where these kidnappers deserved to be. I felt no mercy for them.

> REMEMBER

Chapter 17

Retort

(to answer back, usually sharply)

But it displeased Jonah exceedingly, and he was very

angry.

—*Jonah 4:1*

Weeks after the kidnapping, I felt violated, and my relief that everything had turned out good was turning to anger that it even had to happen. I looked at each person I encountered with suspicion that they could somehow have been involved in the kidnapping. When I came back in to the airport after my first departure, I felt bitter and suspicious. I

REMEMBER

wanted the people involved to pay for what they had done, and I wanted to be the one to dole out punishment.

Those who were put in prison were not the ones who had held a gun to my head or drove off with the children. They only caught the ones who had been staying with them at the time of their rescue. They were beaten before they were arrested, but I wanted to personally take a whip to the people who had been involved with the kidnapping.

When people would stop on the road in front of us and proceed to get out of the vehicle, I was fearful and apprehensive. Maybe they were going to try to get us! I would grip David's leg.

I felt imprisoned in my own house because I no longer had the freedom to come and go as I had been doing. I was not, and to this day am still not,

REMEMBER

allowed to leave with the children by myself in the car as David worried what would happen. I was becoming angry.

When we talk about Jonah in the Bible, we usually think of his disobedience. But in reality, Jonah was a missionary who had seen the fruit of his labor multiplied. After some hesitation, he went to Nineveh, where God had called him, and preached the message God had given him. The people, including the king, responded by fasting, praying, and giving up their evil ways.

However, instead of returning to his own country with exciting reports of the salvation of 120,000 people, he got a bad attitude. Jonah's attitude didn't match his prosperous ministry. He became angry and developed a negative attitude

REMEMBER

toward people and things that he felt were causing his unhappiness.

Jonah was angry with the Ninevites, and these were the very people God had called him to minister to. Ninevah was an evil city. Nahum, a fellow prophet, had pointed out that it was filled with liars, killers, and thieves (Nah. 3:1). Jonah's anger had turned to hatred, and though he preached to them, he really wanted them to be destroyed because they had been so cruel to his people.

This is actually how I started to feel about Haiti. It was an evil place. News reports pointed out this fact daily—that it was indeed filled with liars (corruption), killers, thieves, and, add to the list, kidnappers. Although I continued to minister, I was full of anger and felt as though someone ought to just drop a bomb on Haiti!

REMEMBER

Jonah was also angry with God. He said to God, "I knew it! That is why I didn't want to come in the first place. I knew that you were a loving, compassionate God who would forgive them!" God didn't destroy the people as Jonah had hoped. Jonah asked God to take his life, and then he went outside the city and sat down to see what would happen (Jon. 4:1–5).

I became somewhat angry with God, and I struggled to keep doing what I knew I should do. I began to lose the love and compassion that had once filled my heart for Haiti. I knew I had to forgive those that had hurt me, but it wasn't fair.

Jonah was angry with the vine as well. It had withered and was no longer able to give him shade. Jonah was in a state of confusion and depression. He had found joy in the vine, but then it died. Even

REMEMBER

the little things he might have taken pleasure in were denied him! His attitude, expectations, and comfort level were all out of focus.

His priorities were being questioned and his beliefs challenged. He no longer knew who he was, what he believed, or even what he should do. Having reached the point of despair, he cried out, "It would be better for me to die" (Jon. 4:8).

God wanted to know how Jonah could be upset over the loss of personal pleasure but not over the possible loss, the death, of 120,000 men, women, and children. Jonah didn't care enough to do all he could to save the people of Ninevah but would fuss and work to save a plant.

In the ministry, we are called to be more interested in giving rather than receiving and being comforted. In times of difficulty, it is easy to forget

REMEMBER

this. We come to focus on ourselves, which only leads to anger and frustration. In our work as missionaries, our priority must be obedience to God and service to his people—that is the only way the world is going to be effectively reached for Christ.

> REMEMBER

Chapter 18

Resistance

(effort made to stop or to fight against someone or something)

Whither shall we go up? Our brethren have discouraged our heart.

—*Deuteronomy 1:28*

Simply put, life is pretty hard in Haiti. Political violence, disease, unemployment, corruption, sporadic electricity, and a lack of clean water are constant problems most face on a daily basis. Some refer to Haiti as a missionary graveyard because it is a place where missionaries easily get

REMEMBER

burned out when they see little success in their mission work and become weary facing daily obstacles. Some even leave and refuse to return to Haiti because of bad experiences; they simply say, "There is no hope."

Historically, the term *missionary graveyard* referred to parts of the world where missionaries often died from tropical diseases and unfavorable encounters with the national people. If you went to one of these missionary graveyards, you knew there was a good chance that you were going to die there as a result of sickness or violence.

As a matter of fact, a little over a century ago, some missionaries packed their belongings into coffins instead of suitcases. These one-way missionaries, as they were known, purchased only

REMEMBER

one-way tickets. They were, indeed, committed to a cause.

Over time, with the development of better medicine and with the gradual modernization of many parts of the world, it has become less common for missionaries to die from diseases or violence while on the mission field. Due to this, the term missionary graveyard underwent a change in meaning. Nowadays, it doesn't mean a place where missionaries die, so much as a place where missionaries have a very difficult time achieving success in their mission work.

After the kidnapping, I was somewhat disappointed with the lack of encouragement that we found among some Christians. In fact, we were encouraged to give up and go home. I had a pastor's

REMEMBER

wife tell me that if it were her, she would not go back and take her children to such a place.

So often, we get caught up in an emotional response when we are insulted, and yet in God's Word, there are countless examples of responding by first turning to God.

Many pastors had previously commented they were glad it was not their children or grandchildren that were called. Many people had told me they could not go to Haiti because there was not a Walmart. I wonder, do people realize what a spiritually shallow person this makes them? We can't do God's will because it isn't comfortable?

I have never read in the Bible that everything was going to be easy when we were called to work for God. Evidently, those that said

REMEMBER

this have never considered all that Paul suffered so that the Gospel could be spread.

Here is, in fact, what the Apostle Paul writes in 2 Corinthians 11:23–28: "Are they ministers of Christ? (I speak as a fool) I am more; in labours more abundant, in stripes above measure, in prisons more frequent, in deaths oft. Of the Jews five times received I forty stripes save one. Thrice was I beaten with rods, once was I stoned, thrice I suffered shipwreck, a night and a day I have been in the deep; In journeyings often, in perils of waters, in perils of robbers, in perils by mine own countrymen, in perils by the heathen, in perils in the city, in perils in the wilderness, in perils in the sea, in perils among false brethren; In weariness and painfulness, in watchings often, in hunger and thirst, in fastings often, in cold and nakedness. Beside

REMEMBER

those things that are without, that which cometh upon me daily, the care of all the churches."

David had been on a plane with a man that worked for the World Bank. As they shared about their careers, he told David that working in Haiti was the biggest waste of your life, time, and effort. Haiti was an absolute waste. Now, you can expect this from a secular person but a Christian?

Missions in Haiti was once considered for a large charitable donation. The financial consultant helping to determine where the money would be dispersed was opposed to such a waste of money. He said that Haiti was hopeless and would never get ahead. While, more often than not, this seems to be true, we have to remember that God is working one person at a time.

REMEMBER

My mom has been strong through everything I have faced in Haiti. Not once have I heard her say not to go back. This time was no different; she told me she would not stand in God's way. Whatever he wanted me to do, that was what had to be done. I know her heart was heavy, but she kept her lips closed as to her personal opinion.

REMEMBER

Part III—Reaping

Completed House of Compassion, 2007

> REMEMBER

Chapter 19

Revolution

(a fundamental change in political organization; especially: the overthrow or renunciation of one government or ruler and the substitution of another by the governed; an activity or movement designed to effect fundamental changes in the socioeconomic situation)

But this people hath a revolting and a rebellious heart.
—Jeremiah 5:23

Since 2004 we have experienced many things, starting with the coup d'etat in February 2004. We anxiously followed the news on the

REMEMBER

Internet and watched as former members of the Haitian Army, which had been disbanded, reunited. They named themselves the National Revolutionary Front for the Liberation of Haiti.

On February 5, 2004, they took over the city of Gonaives. This marked the beginning of a revolt against President Aristide. During their takeover of the city, they burned the police station and took the weapons and vehicles from it—items used to continue on with their uprising.

By February 22, the rebels had captured Haiti's second-largest city, Cap-Haitien. David had promised my parents that if they were able to take Cap-Haitien, he would see that the children and I were sent out. I flew out with Davy and Hannah, leaving David behind to take care of our Haitian children and "hold the fort," so to speak.

REMEMBER

As the end of February approached, rebels threatened to take the capital city of Port-au-Prince. This fueled increasing political unrest that was already going on. After a three-week rebellion, Aristide left Haiti on a plane provided by the United States, accompanied by US security personnel. During this time, the rebels took over the capital city.

Shortly after this, an interim government, led by Prime Minister Gérard Latortue and President Boniface Alexandre, was put into power in Haiti. During this time after the coup d'etat, gangs became big in our area of Delmas 31.

I returned to Haiti in March. On the afternoon of March 15, 2005, I was reading in my room after the Haitian children had returned from school. Many of the children were outside playing,

REMEMBER

and gunfire broke out in front of our house. A bullet came through the gate and hit one of the pillars of the carport. The children had run in after weeks of learning to take cover and get down when they heard gunfire nearby.

Gunfire eruptions continued until April 10, 2005. On that day, the gang leader, known to everyone as Grenn Sonnen, was killed during an operation conducted by the interim government. Everyone was hopeful that things would calm down.

Grenn Sonnen was accused of involvement in several murders in the Delmas area. He was believed responsible for the murder of two policemen and the chauffeur of a government executive. The residents of lower Delmas area liked him, and he was even seen as sort of a "hero." They claimed he kept bandits from bothering them.

While gunfire in our area quieted somewhat, instability continued in Haiti. In the early-morning hours of March 31, 2006, we were awakened by strange noises. Initially, we ignored them as we didn't hear the dogs barking. David finally got up to see what was going on, and at that point, he saw heads at the gate. He grabbed his shotgun, stuck it out the window, and cocked it. Upon hearing the sound of the cocking gun, the men took off.

David went out to investigate. At that point, he saw that the generator had been dragged into the road. They had poisoned our German shepherd and left our Rottweiler very sick; we were not sure she would make it. We took some of the bigger

REMEMBER

children, and we all helped David drag the generator back in the yard.

We then hired two security guards. The thieves returned a few nights later, and we were startled awake by the sounds of the security guards firing and the thieves firing back at them. I got Davy and Hannah out of bed and took them to the kitchen area so they would not be wounded by stray bullets.

David went down to get the children on the floor and see what was going on. As we lay on the kitchen floor, I was trembling and praying. I remember Davy asking me if I was scared. I lied and said no; I told him God would take care of us. I didn't want them to be scared too.

REMEMBER

Chapter 20

Reoccurrence

(something that happens again)

Though he fall, he shall not be utterly cast down: for the Lord upholdeth him with his hand.

—Psalm 37:24

| REMEMBER |

Samuel, Davy, and Hannah in front of the ruins of

the presidential palace, 2010

On Tuesday, January 12, 2010, at 4:53 p.m., horror struck once again. A 7.0 catastrophic-magnitude earthquake violently shook Haiti. The epicenter was about sixteen miles west of Port-au-Prince near the area of Léogâne. I was in our church when the shaking began.

REMEMBER

My brother Travis; his wife, Jenny; and their son, Trevor, were here with two other young ladies, Liberty Henegar and Misty Brown, from their church. They had traveled to Haiti to hold a children's crusade at our church.

We were getting ready to start the second night of the children's crusade. My brother was going over his skit and kind of stomping his feet as he began to describe what he would be doing. Coincidentally, at the same time, the ground began to shake. I asked him what in the world he was doing.

It took several seconds to realize what exactly was happening. When I did realize it was an earthquake, I tried to run. I knew I had to save Sam, but I could not get anywhere; I was knocked to the ground by the force of the shaking.

REMEMBER

Hannah was in the church, and I knew she had taken cover under the benches. I remembered Davy and most of the other children were in the yard on their way over. The thing that worried me most was Sammy; I had left him in the bathtub, and David was going to get him out and get him dressed for church.

I started screaming for Sammy; I was crazy with worry. After we got up, I was standing in the back screaming until my friend smacked me in the face to get my attention. I thought of the men on top of the new building we were in the process of constructing. I had greeted them as I went by, but I assumed they had been shaken to their death. By the grace of God, the building still stood, and no one was injured!

REMEMBER

I stepped out to see our house still standing; only the wall had fallen down. Everyone was okay.

By January 24, at least fifty-two aftershocks measuring 4.5 or greater had been reported. Each time, these shakings sent people running and screaming in fear once more. An estimated three million people were affected by the earthquake. Death toll estimates ranged from 100,000 to about 160,000. Haitian government figures ranged from 220,000 to 316,000. Most felt these figures had been deliberately inflated by the Haitian government in order to win sympathy and aid.

The government of Haiti estimated that 250,000 homes and 30,000 buildings for commercial use had collapsed or were severely damaged. Poor housing conditions and no real

REMEMBER

regulations about how structures were to be built caused the death toll to be significant.

The earthquake caused major damage in Port-au-Prince, Jacmel, and other areas in the region. Port-au-Prince's morgues were overwhelmed with thousands of bodies. They were literally carried out of the cities by the dump truck and buried in a mass grave.

Many saw this as an incredibly sad news story; to us, it was real life and people we knew. Good Hope School lost two teachers and two students. Many of the other students were dispersed due to a lack of housing. As rescue attempts waned, supplies, medical care, and sanitation became the priority. Delays in aid distribution led to angry appeals from both aid workers and survivors who were in desperate need. There was looting and

REMEMBER

sporadic violence, which is always sad to observe after such a tragedy.

The earthquake was more stressful in some ways than the kidnapping, due to that fact that its devastating effects lingered on and on. The misery it left was completely devastating for everyone. We were so fortunate that we only had the wall that fell down around the house, but as you can imagine, not having a security wall left us feeling vulnerable. David and the children slept in the living room for three months afterward so that they could get out of the house quicker if another quake struck. David was not sleeping well because he felt like he was on high alert. We were literally overrun with teams coming in to help.

Aid began spoiling people and causing them to form attitudes. There was actually a song on the

REMEMBER

radio that sang about "Monsieur Blanc" or "white guy." It said you should watch out while you are in your yard because that was a great opportunity for them to come after you.

In October of 2010, one of my girls, who I had raised since 2001, felt like the grass was greener on the other side of the wall. She had been in contact with family, and a brother encouraged her to leave. The second girl left in February 2011 after feeling that her ninth grade schoolwork was too hard, and she was tired of being smothered by the rules. The third girl left in March after being reprimanded.

I was completely devastated at the loss of these three girls. I had invested so much time, love, and effort into their lives, and I just didn't see how

REMEMBER

anything good would ever come out of it. I felt like I had wasted ten years of my life!

REMEMBER

Chapter 21

Reaction

(the way someone acts or feels in response to something that happens, is said)

But now it is come upon thee, and thou faintest; it toucheth thee, and thou art troubled.

—Job 4:5

As the school year opened each year, I had a foreboding dread that hung over my head. It had been that way since after my children were kidnapped in October of 2005. Some took this to mean I was ungrateful for what the Lord did for us.

REMEMBER

The truth is I am only human, and I struggle with lots of things.

Initially, I was made to feel that I had to put on my "Miss America" smile and not show any distress over what had happened because it had turned out well. In doing this, I didn't rely on God to be my strength but came to rely on myself to keep any pain, fear, or worry pushed down so that everything would appear to be okay. That way, everyone would be able to see what God had done for us.

I so wish now that I would have had someone to say, "Come apart" and have some rest and get refreshed in the Lord. Instead, I put myself on a course for burnout.

When the third girl left, I was inconsolable. I had been weepy for months, but this was the end of

REMEMBER

my rope; I could not think or process rationally. David booked me on the earliest available flight out of the country to take two weeks to get myself back together. Of course, I felt guilty for leaving the children behind, but I knew I was not helping anyone in my current state. I was completely burned out.

One of the most touching things happened to me at the airport. A young man saw me get out of the truck to get in the boarding line. I was crying and hugging the kids. As I sat waiting to board the plane, he came over to me. He said, "I can see that things are hard for you right now. I saw you had to leave your family, but it is going to be okay." This young man will never know what that meant to me!

Burnout is the result of continual stress over a long period of time. As I said before, we had been

REMEMBER

on high alert—basically since 2004—and our guard was just starting to come down when the earthquake struck. Burnout does not just happen overnight; it creeps up on you. Stress upon stress keeps building without your realizing it. Burnout isn't a psychiatric disorder but a problem, as it will greatly reduce your effectiveness in the ministry in addition to what it does to yourself and your family.

In the Bible, we read about all that Elijah was able to do for God. He told King Ahab that there would be a drought for three and a half years. He ministered to a widow in Zarephath and had victory in the battle on Mount Carmel against the prophets of Baal. He was greatly used by God.

You would think that someone like this would always be encouraged after all that he had seen accomplished for the kingdom of God. But this

REMEMBER

is the same man who we see later out in the wilderness, under a tree suffering from burnout. I knew how he felt. Burnout can occur in the physical, emotional, and spiritual areas of life. Sometimes it affects only one or two of these areas, but it often takes its toll in all three. This is what happened to Elijah. Physically, he became exhausted from running before King Ahab's chariot about twenty-five miles from Mount Carmel to the entrance of Jezreel (1 Kings 18:46). Emotionally, he was drained as we see by his wish to die: "It is enough; now, O Lord, take away my life" (1 Kings 19:4). He was spiritually distraught, which was shown by his words, "I, even I only, am left" (1 Kings 19:10).

    I didn't think committed missionaries could burn out, but I now see the more committed they

REMEMBER

are, the more likely they are to do so. I considered myself to be a determined, committed missionary and didn't think that I could really burn out. I thought I just needed to push myself on, and things would be just fine.

When I would express how I felt to those I was close to, they questioned my spiritual life. Was I praying and reading my Bible like I should? Wouldn't God keep me from burning out?
I was *physically* burned out. Even though I was exhausted every night, I had trouble sleeping. I would fall into a restless sleep with my heart hurting and full of worry about what would happen next. My blood pressure was climbing.

I felt *emotionally* exhausted. I felt drained and used up. The needs of those around me were overwhelming. There was no way that we could

REMEMBER

ever help Haiti. It was not that I didn't want to help people anymore, it was just that I didn't have what it took any longer.

You can't be in the ministry without being involved with people. That in itself is a source of burnout. The "problem people" require much more attention than do the "pleasant people." As a result, you begin to see even good people in a negative light.

You are supposed to be compassionate and caring, so you feel like you can't express the disappointment and frustration that you feel deep down inside. Rather than getting *thank you!* from someone you have helped, you get *what is next?* and a hand extended out.

In order to shield myself, I began to reduce my involvement with others, especially the Haitian

REMEMBER

children who lived with me. I genuinely loved them, but I feared getting close to them again—that I would be crushed again. I actually came to despise people, and my compassion for them was decreasing rather than increasing. I was hard and cynical and saw only the faults in the Haitians.

I felt so much disappointment. Things didn't turn out as I had expected. Unfulfilled expectations make the soil of our heart fertile for seeds of bitterness to spring up and cause extreme depression. It is impossible to continue this way. Our emotional states can't dictate the extent to which our expectations are fulfilled.

At times, I have even slipped into self-pity. I think of the heat in which I am forced to live, no close friends, and difficult living conditions compared to the States. I actually became my own

REMEMBER

source of burnout; I was anxious and blamed myself for failure. I have always had a need to achieve and even based my self-worth on what I saw accomplished.

My human nature tended to be impatient and irritable, and I didn't handle my anger well. All of these traits set me up as a candidate for burnout. Whether or not I was actually ineffective, I felt that way. I began to sense I was becoming the kind of person people do not like. At one time I had been sensitive and caring, but I began to realize I was becoming cold and indifferent. I felt as though I was not accomplishing what I felt God had called me to do.

Spiritually, I was burning out because my faith in God had begun to waiver. I felt like he had

REMEMBER

let me down by allowing bad things to happen to me that he could have prevented.

God called us to do a lot of things for him, but he didn't call us to burn out or drop out. My one-time motto had been "I would rather burn out than rust out." I now see the wisdom in pacing myself. I want what Paul said in 2 Timothy 4:7 to be true for myself: I want to finish well!

REMEMBER

Chapter 22

Recovery

(the act or process of returning to a normal state after a period of difficulty)

O spare me, that I may recover strength, before I go hence, and be no more.

—Psalm 39:13

I have heard that missionaries who are suffering from burnout to the point that they leave their field of labor are unlikely to return. I know that this would have been the case for me if we would have listened to many well-meaning people

REMEMBER

who told us to get out of here after some of the events that I have previously shared.

For this very fact, I am glad that I never gave up and went home after incidents that put a lot of stress on me. It would have been so easy to slip back into an easier life and forget about what God had asked me to do—or even give an excuse that I tried, but it didn't work out.

In the summer of 2011, David and I attended a personal retreat in Canada where we were alone with a host and counselor. It was a week of intense counseling and direction; I learned many things to help me in the future, and learning to set realistic goals was one. I had wanted to see the whole country of Haiti be saved and have revival. I can't do this on my own, and I can't force others to help

REMEMBER

me. I have to pace myself and wait for God to provide the ministry with workers.

I can't blame myself for everything that goes wrong. After all, Judas was a disciple of Jesus. Judas followed him, heard his teachings, and saw the miracles, and yet, in the end, he betrayed the Son of God. I have come to see that some people are just going to take the hard road in spite of everything you have taught them.

The alternative to pacing myself, resting, and refusing to take the blame for everything that goes wrong is that it will make me a miserable person. When I am miserable, it has a negative effect on those around me as well.

> REMEMBER

Chapter 23

Renewal

(the state of being made new, fresh, or strong again)

And be not conformed to this world: but be ye transformed by the renewing of your mind, that ye may prove what is that good, and acceptable, and perfect, will of God.

—*Romans 12:2*

In the fall of 2011, we were blessed to attend a ministers' retreat with the Bible Holiness Ministerial Fellowship. While there, I felt God speak to me through Reverend Jeff Mayo. He preached about the Apostle Paul. Because of the

REMEMBER

things that he faced and overcame by the grace of God, he was a man that men would listen to.

If anyone was a candidate for burnout, it was the Apostle Paul. In Acts 20, we read about his preaching all night in Troas and then leaving by ship early the next day. There is no mention of his taking any time to sleep or rest. Although we have no record of it, this was probably not the only time that Paul conducted all night meetings.

It seems that he had an endless amount of energy. His difficult experiences, many of which are listed in 2 Corinthians 11:23–29, would have been more than enough to cause the average person to have a nervous breakdown.

Paul also refers to his care of all the churches on a daily basis. The care of just one church pushes many people into burnout. The

REMEMBER

number of churches Paul cared for isn't certain, but there is no evidence from the scriptures that he ever suffered physical, emotional, or spiritual burnout. How did he avoid it? What was his secret? In the book of Acts and in his epistles, Paul shares with us many striking statements that sustained him in the worst of situations: "None of these things move me" (Acts 20:24).

> REMEMBER

Chapter 24

Reevaluate

(to judge anew the value or condition of someone or something in a careful and thoughtful way)

Lord, make me to know mine end, and the measure of my days, what it is: that I may know how frail I am.
—*Psalm 39:4*

In 2012, I felt that I was coming out of the clouds, so to speak. I felt as though I had been in a fog, and it was starting to lift, and I could see clearly again.

I came to the conclusion—after much reevaluation of my priorities—that I have to pace

REMEMBER

myself. At times, I have forced myself to push on despite fatigue, whether it was physical, spiritual, or even emotional. I now realize that I have to rest more physically. Things will get done, maybe not as fast as I would like them to, but they will get done. It doesn't all have to be done today.

Spiritually, we have seen the positive effects of being out of Haiti a little more often so that we are able to refuel our spiritual tanks, be it through missionary conferences or ministerial retreats. There are benefits of spending time with like-minded believers who will encourage you to press on toward the mark.

Emotionally, I have come to the reality that I can't force the Haitian children to love me no matter how much I love them. I have had to pull back in some respects because I realize that in the

REMEMBER

end, some choose their biological family over those who really have their best interests at heart.

I realized I have to put my biological children first. To do this, I have to think of my own health because they need me. I have to keep myself from being an emotional basket case. If that means being less involved with those who are apt to hurt me, then that is what I have to do so that I can continue to be strong for my own children and those who choose to be part of my family.

Some have commented on the withdrawal they see and feel it isn't fair. They want me to continue giving even though I receive nothing because they say that is the Christian thing to do. Ironically, the ones to notice are the ones who give me the most problems and show no genuine care or concern about me as a person.

Chapter 25

Restoration

(the act of bringing back something that existed before)

He restoreth my soul: he leadeth me in the paths of righteousness for his name's sake.

—*Psalm 23:3*

REMEMBER

I have come to think differently about the adversity that I face in Haiti as well as in the ministry. I am blessed beyond measure. It is nothing that I did to earn or deserve all the many blessings that have come my way.

It is only by the grace of God that I am where I am today. Grace is a concept that I failed to actually understand until recently. I have been in church since I was a child and never strayed too far.

My grandpa Jones spent his life pushing God away. He said he was not worthy. He is a World War II veteran who obviously saw a lot of horrible things that he never completely opened up about and shared. We went to see Grandpa one day in November of 2015. As he lay in confusion in his nursing home bed, he saw David. Grandpa began to weep and said that he was a lost cause; he had been

REMEMBER

in the war and had done bad things. But thankfully, a few weeks earlier he had been in his right mind and spoke to Darryl Meadow, and we felt that he had made things right with God. Grandpa had gone through life feeling unworthy, but God says he is worthy, and, in his infinite grace, he keeps reaching to him.

I have always appreciated how the Haitians use the word *grace* nearly every day, in that anything they accomplish, or if they are even still here on the earth, have food to eat, and have air to breathe, is only by the grace of God.

Grace, for me in my life, has been God's kindness that daily draws me closer to him, no matter what I have done or been through. Often I do not have the grace to continue to reach out to those who have hurt or offended me. I leave them alone,

REMEMBER

but thank God, he does not leave me alone; he continues to seek me out in his kindness.

The following poem could be considered harsh, but I have adopted it as my mantra:

I am a soldier in the army of my God.
The Lord Jesus Christ is my commanding officer.
The Holy Scripture is my code of conduct.
Faith, prayer and the Word are my weapons of warfare.
I have been taught by the Holy Spirit, trained by experience,
tried by adversity, and tested by fire.
I am a volunteer in this army, and I am enlisted for eternity.
I will not get out, sell out, be talked out, or pushed out.

REMEMBER

I am faithful, reliable, capable, and dependable.

If my God needs me, I am there. I am a soldier.

I am not a baby. I do not need to be pampered,

petted,

primed up, pumped up, picked up, or pepped up. I

am a soldier.

No one has to call me, remind me, write me, visit

me, entice me, or lure me.

I am a soldier. I am not a wimp. I am in place,

saluting my King,

obeying His orders, praising His name, and building

His kingdom!

No one has to send me flowers, gifts, food, cards, or

candy, or give me handouts. I do not need to be

cuddled, cradled, cared for, or catered to. I am

committed. I can't have my feelings hurt badly

enough to turn me around. I can't be discouraged

REMEMBER

enough to turn me aside. I can't lose enough to cause me to quit. When Jesus called me into this army, I had nothing. If I end up with nothing, I will still come out ahead. I will win. My God has and will continue to supply all of my need. I am more than a conqueror. I will always triumph. I can do all things through Christ. The devil can't defeat me. People can't disillusion me. Weather can't weary me. Sickness can't stop me. Battles can't beat me. Money can't buy me. Governments can't silence me, and hell can't handle me. I am a soldier. Even death can't destroy me. For when my Commander calls me from His battlefield, He will promote me to captain and then allow me to rule with Him. I am a soldier in the army, and I'm marching claiming victory.

REMEMBER

I will not give up. I will not turn around.

I am a soldier, marching heaven bound.

Here I stand! Will you stand with me?

Unknown author

> REMEMBER

Chapter 26

Recognize

(to accept or be aware that something is true or exists)

To the weak became I as weak, that I might gain the weak: I am made all things to all men, that I might by all means save some.
—*1 Corinthians 9:22*

Through tough times in Haiti, I have had to recognize or literally think differently about what all has happened. I had resented the many things that caused pain and suffering. I had to recognize the chaos that we had been through. I came to see that it had caused growth personally, as well as in

REMEMBER

our ministry, that would not have occurred if not for these rough times.

We studied about many things in missiology class at Ozark Bible Institute, but nothing can prepare you for the stress that you will feel culturally. Again, recognizing these factors and seeing how to deal with them will help you to be able to go on. Some people believe that they can adapt to anything, even continual stress, without it hurting them. The truth is it just does not work that way.

Over the years, I had observed that some of the effective missionaries in Haiti, who had been here for years, were not as involved personally with the people as I had imagined that a missionary would need to be. I now see that the more you involve yourself, the more stress you may feel.

REMEMBER

There is a different value system between two cultures. The greater the difference between where you come from and where you are a missionary can cause a great deal of stress. I really thought that this would not be a big deal, but it is something that bothers me to this day.

For example, in Haiti, there are different values placed on cleanliness. I am always amused that the Haitians think we do not know how to do laundry because we use a washing machine. Our socks are never as pure white as theirs are that are washed by hand. They find that disgusting. I explain that no one will see it. (Yet, it does not bother them to urinate on the side of the road where many will be walking.)

REMEMBER

We, as Americans, are very prompt; Haitians not so much. It frustrates me when they do not respect others by showing up late. They never see what the big deal is. Our sense of responsibility is much different as well. When you ask someone why something happened, a common response here is that it was not their fault.

Communication itself is another stress factor. Learning the meanings of words and rules of grammar are only a small part of being able to communicate effectively with the people you minister to. The whole way of thinking, the common knowledge base, and the use of nonverbal cues are necessary and come only with great familiarity with the culture.

For example, Haitians do have many nonverbal cues that we are able to pick up and know

REMEMBER

what they mean. However, after all this time, I do not get their sense of humor; they do not get ours either. My children can laugh at the Haitian jokes and don't understand why I can't get them. Being raised here has definitely had an impact on my children.

Temperament is another stress factor. Haitians are very laid back. My temperament is very different: I am high strung. They never understand my sense of urgency to see a task done. After all, "it will get done when it gets done."

I can say, however, that after living in the Haitian culture this long, I will never be the same. Though I never feel completely at home in Haiti, when I am in the United States, I am no longer completely at home there either. Americans seem

REMEMBER

spoiled to me with all their comforts and materialism.

A lot can be done to decrease culture stress and make it manageable. Stress is a part of life, and everyone learns how to manage it or suffers the consequences. It is difficult to become at home in two cultures, and it typically takes a very long time to do so successfully.

The factors that help cope with stress are summarized in the three qualities Paul mentioned in 1 Corinthians 13, which are faith, hope, and love.

My faith in God has sustained me through many difficult situations. Knowing that God has called me to do work for him in Haiti, and that he has always been there and will be there in the future, is an encouragement when times get tough.

REMEMBER

Rather than feeling helpless, I can put my hope in God. I have not only the hope of eternity with God but also hope in my future, knowing that he has good plans for me, and he will help me cope.

Finally, having both God's love and the love of his people to give me support in the stressful situations that I face daily will help me cope. I know God loves me in spite of the countless mistakes I make every day. Being a mother has helped me understand God's love for us. I always love my children no matter what; it is just that sometimes I am disappointed in the choices they make.

| REMEMBER |

Chapter 27

Reap

(to get something, such as a reward, as a result of something that you have done)

They that sow in tears shall reap in joy.

—Psalm 126:5

Miriam's graduation, 2014

REMEMBER

Missionaries are all victims of Satan's persecution, but that does not mean missionaries need to have a victim mentality. As we see in the New Testament, Jesus refused to adopt the victim mentality when he was persecuted on various occasions. Likewise, there is no need for missionaries to develop such a mentality. Missionaries can develop a victor mentality because, though they may be victims, they are also victors through the faithfulness of Jesus Christ, who helps overcome.

A victor mentality is a positive way of thinking. It is a mentality of viewing the world from a positive perspective. Rather than seeing persecution as negative, it is seen as a chance to

REMEMBER

learn something that will, in turn, make us a better person.

If we focus on negativity all the time, it is easy to fall into the mentality of being a victim. That is why it is important to hide God's word in our heart so that we can meditate on it.

David and I decided not to adopt the victim mentality. The benefits we are reaping from our decision to press on in Haiti are great.

The kidnapping was harder on Miriam than the other two children, I guess because she was older and realized what was going on more so than Davy and Hannah. To this day, she still does not like to talk about it.

Miriam overcame the obstacles in her life, and she graduated from high school in 2014. She was denied a student visa three times, but after

REMEMBER

getting serious in prayer, her visa was granted. In the fall of 2015, she started Bible school in Pennsylvania.

> REMEMBER

Chapter 28

Relinquish

(to give up something: to give something, such as power, control, or possession to another person or group)

For this child I prayed; and the Lord hath given me my petition which I asked of him: Therefore also I have lent him to the Lord; as long as he liveth he shall be lent to the Lord.

—1 Samuel 1:27–28

REMEMBER

Hannah, Cap-Haitien, 2015

Davy has such a heart for Haiti. He does not encounter the stress of the cultural difference because it is his culture as well. He has always been fluent in Creole and, in fact, spoke Creole much better than English until he started school. I can't express how proud I am of the heart that Davy has for the Haitian people.

REMEMBER

It has, in fact, been my prayer since Davy was a baby that the Lord would use his life to bring glory to God. I knew this might mean that Davy would have to make sacrifices in order to do God's will.

Hannah was a different story. The aftereffects of the kidnapping had me so bound that I was opposed to her doing anything for God. I just wanted her to be able to live a "normal" life with a family and such. I asked God not to even look her way. The ministry was just too hard, and I didn't want to see her have to face even a portion of what I had encountered. It was just too painful.

After I began to heal, I knew that this had been a wrong attitude. I had named Hannah after the prophet Samuel's mother in the Bible. Of all the women in the Bible, I find her to be the most

REMEMBER

admirable—a woman who promised God that if he would give her what her heart desired, she would, in turn, give the child back to God.

Hannah also has a heart for Haiti. She has so many Haitian ways that she adopted from being raised here that I worry how she will do if she ever goes back to live in the States.

Davy and Hannah are not comfortable with their American peer group. They see them as shallow and self-centered. Davy and Hannah have literally lived among the many children we are raising. I often tell them that when they grow up, they can tell everyone they were raised in an orphanage.

Chapter 29

Rock

(foundation, support, refuge)

He only is my rock and my salvation; he is my defence; I shall not be greatly moved.

—*Psalm 62:2*

REMEMBER

Hannah, Port Salut, 2012

I can look back in my life and see that Jesus is the Rock that was always there leading and guiding me.

I know from experience that nothing is impossible with God. He has never left me or forsaken me. I am so thankful that I was raised in a

REMEMBER

Christian home. I knew from the time I was a child that God would be my Rock. And now I can tell you he is my Rock, and at the end of my days, I will tell you he was always my Rock.

Because he is my Rock, I will not be moved. I know that in the past I struggled, but, in fact, that has made me stronger. Now as I face problems, they do not move me as they have in times past; I know that God is faithful, and I do not need to worry.

REMEMBER

Chapter 30

Recruit

(to fill up the number of, as an army, with new members)

And he said to them all, If any man will come after me,

let him deny himself,

and take up his cross daily, and follow me.

—*Luke 9:23*

REMEMBER

Davy and Oliver

When I was a kid, there used to be a commercial on TV that was recruiting people for the Peace Corps. It proclaimed the Peace Corps was the toughest job you'll ever love. I think the same could be said of the ministry. It is a tough job, but I love it.

REMEMBER

I always try to encourage young people to choose to work for God instead of seeking after wealth and fame. Both of them can cause you to lose your soul in the end, whereas in the ministry, you can take other souls with you to heaven.

While going through some of the hard times, I might not have been able to say this, but as David and I started to see some of the fruits of our labor, I can tell you it was worth it all. Live and work for Jesus—that is all that will matter in the end.

REMEMBER

REMEMBER

Photos taken of the children shortly before the kidnapping

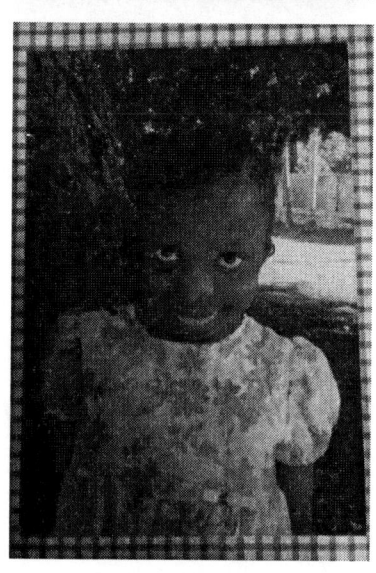

> REMEMBER

Articles by the Associated Press

A couple of years ago, we were visiting a church that had inserted part of the following article in the Sunday bulletin. Davy and Hannah said, "Look, Mom, did you know we were famous?"

They had no idea that their story had appeared in newspapers around the world. I then shared with them that the story had also appeared on news stations, and their grandparents had recounted what had happened on a Tulsa news channel.

I told them that Grandma Darlin (my mom) had saved articles from various newspapers, and so forth, in a box for them. They were amazed that people all over had read and known about it.

REMEMBER

Three Kidnapped Children Rescued in Haiti

By Alfred de Montesquiou, Associated Press

Monday October 31, 2005, at 11:00 p.m. ET

Police rescued two kidnapped children and a foster child of an American missionary couple during a raid on an apartment in Haiti's capital, officials said Monday.

Police said Hannah Lloyd, 3, her brother David, 5, and their Haitian foster sister Miriam Merenvil, 7, were unharmed.

The children of Pentecostal minister David Lloyd and his wife, Alicia, were abducted after they left school on Friday and rescued the next day. Police

REMEMBER

said they delayed in publicizing the crime until Monday to avoid jeopardizing an investigation.

Lloyd, of Claremore, Okla., told The Associated Press in a telephone interview that while the children weren't injured, "my little girl is still very scared."

He said the older children told him that at one point, the kidnappers threatened Hannah that they would shoot her unless she stopped crying.

Police said the kidnapping occurred shortly after Alicia Lloyd picked up the children. Several armed men dressed as police officers in a van marked "police" cut them off in downtown traffic, seized the children and sped away.

Police traced the men to an apartment building in the volatile Delmas neighborhood and raided the

REMEMBER

property on Saturday, freeing the children and arresting seven suspects, including a former police officer, said Michael Lucius, the head of Haiti's Judicial Police.

"We operated very fast and no one was hurt," Lucius said.

He said police were investigating if the other six suspects were current or former police officers.

The children were the latest victims of a surge of kidnappings that have added to insecurity ahead of the first elections since the February 2004 ouster of President Jean-Bertrand Aristide. Police reported more than 50 kidnappings in September.

Lloyd said someone phoned him asking for a $350,000 ransom for the children's release, but he said he couldn't be sure if it was the captors.

REMEMBER

He said the captors allowed him to speak with the children by phone several times before they were freed. During one conversation, the children said they were fed a pack of cheese puffs and a soda for dinner.

Lloyd, who runs the "Missions in Haiti" charity with his wife, said he wouldn't leave Haiti. The charity helps raise 21 Haitian foster children.

"It's been a pretty rough year, but we feel this is where God wants us to be, and we will stay with our mission," Lloyd said.

> **REMEMBER**

BBC NEWS

Haiti Kidnap Children Freed Alive

Story from *BBC News*

Tuesday, November 1, 2005, at 11:23 GMT

Three children snatched in a Haiti shanty town at the weekend have been freed in a rescue operation.

The son and daughter of a US missionary were kidnapped along with their Haitian foster sister by a gang dressed in police uniforms.

They were rescued by genuine police officers 24 hours later in the Delmas area of Haiti's capital Port-au-Prince.

REMEMBER

Much of Haiti is enduring a breakdown of law and order, including a wave of kidnappings and violent gun crime.

Hannah Lloyd, aged three, and her elder brother David, five, had been picked up from school by their mother when they were intercepted by a group of men driving a van.

Foster sister Miriam Merenvil, aged seven, was also in the car.

Wielding guns, the men grabbed the children from their car and fled.

Haitian police quickly traced the children's captors, raiding a residential apartment a day after the children were seized.

No-one was harmed during the raid, police said, and seven suspected gang members were arrested.

REMEMBER

One of those held was reported to be a former police officer.

The children's father, David Lloyd, said he received phone calls demanding ransom payments during the 24 hours the three children were held.

One unidentified caller asked for a payment of $350,000 (£198,000), Mr. Lloyd told the Associated Press.

Mr. Lloyd, an evangelical minister from Claremore, Oklahoma, runs a charity that cares for 21 Haitian foster children.

He plans to stay in Haiti with his wife, Alicia, who helps run the charity, Mr. Lloyd told AP.

"It's been a pretty rough year, but we feel this is where God wants us to be, and we will stay with our mission."

REMEMBER

Elections due

Violence linked to poverty and the lack of a strong central government has mushroomed in Haiti since the ouster of former President Jean-Bertrand Aristide in 2004.

More than 800 people have died in violence during 2005 despite the presence of 7,000 United Nations troops in the country.

Journalists and foreigners have become targets, with a rash of killings and kidnappings turning much of the capital into a no-go area.

Democratic elections are scheduled for December, but there are fears that flawed polls could prompt fresh violence.

> **REMEMBER**

Broken Saints an Alabaster Box

By Pastor Joseph Chambers, Paw Creek Ministries

When the news came to me from Alicia Lloyd's mother that the children had been kidnapped, I was instantly a broken soul. I fell apart emotionally. I was ashamed of myself as I tried to tell my staff and then call everybody I could reach to pray. This old clay jar was broken and out of it came prayer like a river of groaning in the Spirit. It was not long before the Holy Spirit said to me, "The work is done." A good number of other prayer warriors have told me similar stories. When the vessel of a genuine saint of God is broken by the Spirit of intercession and prayer, nothing can come from that vessel but Divine activity that brings God into human affairs. I pray that this great mission story

REMEMBER

will never be forgotten and that our God can possess an army of broken vessels.

I dare not call us the "alabaster box" because that was Jesus Christ alone. But we are His "clay vessels," and He desires for us to be a replica of Himself in our own lesser way. The smitten saint cannot be denied of his Biblical request or burden that he pours out of his broken soul. The soul of man is the real seat of the person, and it is many times more powerful to speak of a smitten soul than of broken human emotions. Our human emotions can be broken by many things of little value. The very heart or soul of a man is a deep reservoir out of which can flow the fullness of absolute surrender and passion for a cause that is wholly the needs of others. That's the kind of passion which smote the Rock of Christ upon the cross and opened a

REMEMBER

fountain of salvation to the whole world. We can share this deep suffering and fill up the redemption and deliverance of broken lives.

The garden of Gethsemane was the beginning of the "broken alabaster box." This great time of sorrow has always been a mystery beyond my full understanding. "Sweat was as it were great drops of blood," "He was heard in that He feared," and "Let this cup pass from me, nevertheless not my will but thine." Those words are too high for me. But the depth of this night was the brokenness that prepared the sacrifice to be offered. It was all part of the Father's plan to draw from the fountain of His life a perfect cup of sorrow. When it was finished, the Son of God could descend into upper Sheol and deliver four thousand years of faith with His message of eternal grace. A guilty, common thief

REMEMBER

could be perfectly converted right beside the "Smitten Rock" hanging on a tree. The spikenard from the alabaster box had touched the heart of the Creator and redemption was complete. "Yet it pleased the Lord (His Father) to bruise Him; He (the Father) hath put Him to grief when thou (the Father) shall make His soul an offering for sin...He (the Father) shall see the travail of His Son and shall be satisfied" (Isaiah 53:10–11).

Now it is our time to be smitten. Only broken saints that joyously share His suffering and sorrows with soul-rending prayer and travail can open the door to revival. When our Great God has a supernatural design, when He moves to reveal Himself and changes lives, and even changes a society for His Kingdom, first He moves upon His saints. He breaks them to travail by His Spirit in them, and

REMEMBER

then great grace fills His church, His chosen geography, and there is an awakening. It cannot and will not happen until there are broken vessels of great intercession. Neither can it fail when God has chosen His surrendered saints and they willingly give themselves to Him.

These great times of refreshing cannot be manipulated by fleshly campaigns and great displays of religion. Religion begets more religion and enough religion can kill everything spiritual. Many great revivals have been effectively destroyed by the dominating forces of religion. Broken saints that yearn to follow the "Smitten Rock," and that seek no prominence for flesh, will soon discover that God is searching for them just as surely as they

REMEMBER

are searching for Him. Remember the prophet that said, "For the eyes of the LORD run to and fro throughout the whole earth, to shew himself strong in the behalf of them whose heart is perfect toward him" (2 Chronicles 16:9a). The Gospel writer James said, "Draw nigh to God, and he will draw nigh to you" (James 4:8).

We are blessed to be at the door of revival. Wickedness has made itself known in an overarching sweep of our world. That cannot happen without the sharp attention of the Sovereign Creator. He is not absent from His creation but always in perfect preparation for His Divine plans. The greatest thing we can ever do is to be totally His, fully surrender to His great will, and set apart from an evil world that would draw us into its dark plans, and blind us to His next great revelation.

REMEMBER

Surrender to Him and watch and wait for what He is about to do. Be ready to weep as your soul is moved for a world that is desperate for God.

Miriam, Davy, and Hannah 2006

REMEMBER

REMEMBER

-

For more information:

www.missionsinhaiti.com

Like us on Facebook

Missions in Haiti, Inc.

REMEMBER